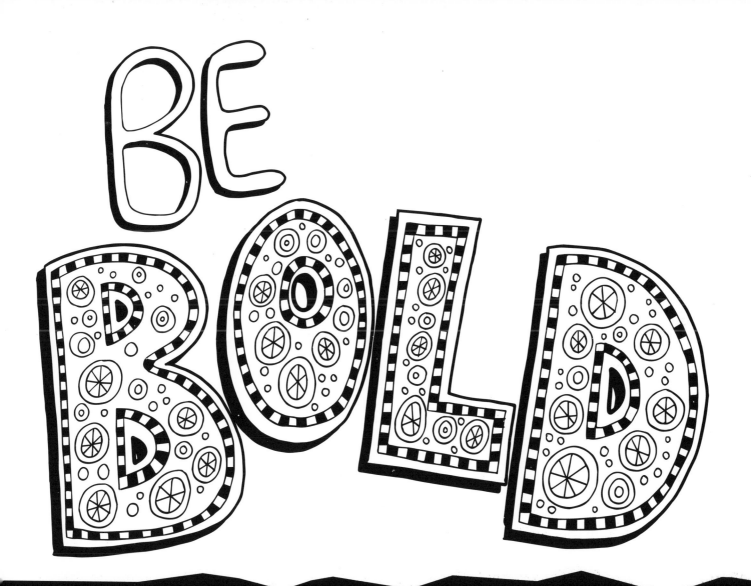

BE BOLD

A COLORING DEVOTIONAL BY ELLEN ELLIOTT

Tyndale House Publishers, Inc.
Carol Stream, Illinois

Visit Tyndale online at www.tyndale.com.

TYNDALE and Tyndale's quill logo are registered trademarks of Tyndale House Publishers, Inc.

Be Bold: A Coloring Devotional

Text and art copyright © 2017 by Ellen Matkowski. All rights reserved.

Designed by Jacqueline L. Nuñez

Edited by Sarah Rubio

Published in association with the literary agency of Prospect Agency, 551 Valley Rd., PMB 377, Upper Montclair, NJ 07043.

Scripture quotations are taken from the *Holy Bible*, New Living Translation, copyright © 1996, 2004, 2015 by Tyndale House Foundation. Used by permission of Tyndale House Publishers, Inc., Carol Stream, Illinois 60188. All rights reserved.

For information about special discounts for bulk purchases, please contact Tyndale House Publishers at csresponse@tyndale.com or call 800-323-9400.

ISBN 978-1-4964-1787-9

Printed in China

23 22 21 20 19 18 17
7   6   5   4   3   2   1

For my bold friend Mindy

BE STILL

Be still, and know that I am God!

—Psalm 46:10

There's a stretch of land between Texas and North Dakota nicknamed "Tornado Alley." The people who live there know the fierce destruction that tornadoes can cause and make provisions accordingly—hiding in basements and storm cellars, even wearing bike helmets. When the meteorologists get nervous and the sirens start to blare, the residents of Tornado Alley take cover!

Tornadoes can rip apart cars, houses, and schools. But at the center of a cyclone's vortex of dust, litter, hail—and sometimes even cows!—it's a different story. Although the outer winds of a tornado can reach up to three hundred miles per hour, the eye of the storm is mostly still.

Sometimes our lives can feel like a twister, spinning out of control. We are faced with conflict, mishaps, and heartache. We race to keep up with other people's expectations. We try to make everyone happy. The harder we try to control life's whirlwind, the more exhausted we become.

But God tells us to be still and know that He is God. *He* is in control, not us. If we put God at the center of our lives, then—no matter how much chaos is swirling around us—we will have stillness and peace.

BELIEVE IN MIRACLES

Jesus . . . said, "Humanly speaking, it is impossible. But with God everything is possible."

—Matthew 19:26

When you hear the word *miracle*, what is the first image that springs to mind?

God parting the Red Sea for Moses and the Israelites?
Jesus walking on water?
Lazarus being raised from the dead?
Jesus feeding five thousand people with just two fish and five loaves of bread?

Those were some pretty fantastic miracles. But God's miracles are still happening every day, all around us. His miraculous gifts can be big and amazing, but they can also come in small, quiet packages.

A miracle could be

a change of heart,
forgiveness between friends,
the strength to overcome a lifelong fear,
repentance for hurting a classmate's feelings, or
a yearning heart asking for salvation.

Yes, with God, everything is possible!
Let's notice God's miracles today, both big and small.

CHOOSE JOY

Don't be dejected and sad, for the joy of the Lord is your strength!

—Nehemiah 8:10

Are you a fashionista who loves opening the closet every morning? Do you throw on a flowing dress and delicate ballet flats one day and then reach for your military jacket and steel-toed combat boots the next? On other days, do you grab your polka-dot, knee-high socks; pink cowboy boots; and flashing Christmas-tree sweater to match your funky mood? Do you sometimes decide to stay in your pajamas all day long, just because you can?

Just like you choose your clothing, you can make a decision about your attitude every single morning. You can choose to put on grumpiness and entitlement, roaring out of the house like a cranky lion. You can decide to wear your irritability all day like a glove, fixated on your displeasure.

Or, instead, you can choose joy and gratitude. You can remember your blessings from God and wear them proudly. No matter what gorgeous outfit your body is clothed in, a joyful heart is what will really make you beautiful.

But even if you do choose poorly and start the day off with an unthankful heart, isn't it wonderful to know that you can always change your mind at any point in the day? You can turn to God and put on a new attitude. It's never too late for a change of heart.

FOR GOOD

"I know the plans I have for you," says the LORD. "They are plans for good and not for disaster, to give you a future and a hope."

—Jeremiah 29:11

Wouldn't it be nice to have a script for your life?

That way, whenever life gets scary or confusing, you could pull the script off the shelf and find out exactly what you're supposed to do next. Want to know whether you're in a comedy or a tragedy? Just take a look at the script.

You would know how to act in certain scenes—whether to stay or go, laugh or cry, try or quit. You would know exactly which movie to see, which boots to wear, and who will take you to prom. You could sidestep traps of heartache and disappointment with ease.

Well, God has already written the story of your life.

He knows the way things are going to turn out. He has made plans for your life, and they are good! God's plans for you include joy, adventure, and love. Our faith grows as we trust Him one day at a time, one minute at a time. Difficulties and problems are going to happen, but your story does not end in despair. Because you know Christ, your life is not a tragedy. It is a love story.

You don't have to worry about your future, because He is holding your story in the palm of His hand.

I KNOW THE PLANS I HAVE FOR YOU.

JEREMIAH 29:11

BELIEVE WHO GOD SAYS YOU ARE

See how very much our Father loves us, for he calls us his children, and that is what we are!

—1 John 3:1

If you were a car, what bumper stickers would be stuck on you?
Would they say . . .

Daughter?	Teacher's pet?	Black sheep?
Sister?	Social butterfly?	Drama queen?
Friend?	Nerd?	Neat freak?
Honor student?	Rebel?	Slob?
Dog walker?	Good girl?	
Cheerleader?	Class clown?	

Who gave you these labels? Do you like them?

We're often labeled by our family, friends, teachers, classmates, and even strangers. Sometimes, we give labels to ourselves. Many labels are simple facts, like *daughter* or *sister*. Others, like *neat freak* and *slob*, or *pretty* and *ugly*, are merely opinions.

You get to choose whether you stick a label on yourself or peel it off and throw it away. The labels that you wear will affect how you treat yourself and the people around you. So whose labels are you accepting?

Human opinions are often based on false or superficial things. What really matters is the true identity that God has bestowed on you. He has called you His beloved child. You are precious to Him—part of His family.

The world's flimsy labels will fade and peel away, but your identity as God's child will remain forever.

TOUGH BUT WORTH IT

We can rejoice, too, when we run into problems and trials, for we know that they help us develop endurance. And endurance develops strength of character, and character strengthens our confident hope of salvation.

—Romans 5:3-4

What builds character?

Living a cushy life?
Getting everything you want?
Never having to stand up for your beliefs?
Instantly being good at anything new that you try?
Never experiencing loss, sadness, frustration, or disappointment?

As nice as those things might sound, the answer is obviously no.

The Bible says that trials build our endurance (our "stick-with-it-ness"), which develops our character, which leads to solid faith in God. The truth is that the life events that shape us most are often made of rough stuff. When everything is going smoothly, we have a tendency to glide through life, relying on our own strength. However, when we are faced with seemingly insurmountable hurdles, we are faced with reality. We cannot do it on our own! We need Jesus.

As tough as your character-building lessons are, you can look back and be grateful for the challenges that God has helped you face. They shape your faith and make you into the person God created you to be.

HE KNOWS YOU

I knew you before I formed you in your mother's womb.
Before you were born I set you apart
and appointed you as my prophet to the nations.

—Jeremiah 1:5

You walk into a crowded cafeteria, holding your tray of food. Your hands are trembling a bit, and you try to keep the tray steady so nobody will notice. You try to play it cool, but your eyes dart around the room, searching for a familiar face.

You could sit at that empty table by yourself, but you'd really like to eat lunch with a friend. You keep scanning the room as you walk slowly, hoping to hear someone say, "Hey there! Come on over!"

Suddenly, you see a hand wave to you.

Relief.

As humans, we long to be special. We want to be known by someone else, to be thought about, to be appreciated. When we are excluded or forgotten, the sting can be painful. But even if we end up shunned by everyone else, our Lord will never reject us.

God doesn't just recognize you; He knows you intimately. As your Creator, He knows you better than anyone else does. He created you, and He doesn't make mistakes. In fact, He thinks you are terrific!

With God, you never have to sit alone.

GOD'S THOUGHTS

"My thoughts are nothing like your thoughts," says the LORD.
"And my ways are far beyond anything you could imagine."

—Isaiah 55:8

How does our human understanding compare to that of our mighty God?

A crayon drawing versus the *Mona Lisa*
A pebble versus the moon
A tiny minnow versus a great blue whale
A speck of sand versus Mount Rushmore
A drop of water versus the Pacific Ocean

But even these comparisons don't do justice to the magnitude and mightiness of God's perfect will and ways.

God sees beyond what our human minds can comprehend. His thoughts and plans are *huge*, stretching into heaven and eternity. Our view is a tiny glimpse of a single moment, but His view is the full expanse of time.

We have no idea what wonders our Lord has planned. But we can trust that His ways are perfect and He knows what He is doing in the universe—and in our lives.

My ways are FAR BEYOND ANYThiNG You could iMAGiNE.

Isaiah 55:8

YOUR SHEPHERD

Acknowledge that the Lord is God!
  He made us, and we are his.
  We are his people, the sheep of his pasture.

—Psalm 100:3

In 2004, a headstrong sheep named Shrek made headlines in New Zealand.

Shrek was a Merino sheep, a domesticated breed that needs to be shorn yearly because its wool never stops growing. If these sheep aren't clipped regularly, they can face several difficulties, including skin infection, visual impairment, trouble moving, and heat exhaustion.

One day, Shrek decided that he was done being shorn. He hid in a cave from his farmer for six years. *Six years!* Can you imagine what Shrek looked like when he was finally caught? Yep—like a massive, dirty ball of yarn.

Shrek became a national celebrity in New Zealand and was shorn on television, raising money for charity. The shearers removed sixty pounds of wool, enough to make twenty suits. Shrek went home to live with his farmer, who kept a close eye on the wandering sheep after that.

Some of us are very stubborn, just like Shrek. We think we know what's best for us, so we set out on our own path—away from our Shepherd's watchful eye. But that's when we can get ourselves into big trouble! We need our Shepherd.

No matter how headstrong and dirty and messy we are, God still loves us passionately. He would search in a million caves until He found us.

If you are running from God right now, maybe it's time to let Him find you.

We are His People, the SHEEP of His PASTURE.

Psalm 100:3

HE WILL FINISH HIS WORK IN YOU

*I am certain that God, who began the good work within you,
will continue his work until it is finally finished on the day when
Christ Jesus returns.*

—Philippians 1:6

Do you have any of the following in your closet?

An incomplete painting
A half-knitted scarf
A puzzle you shoved aside to finish later
A shirt with a missing button that hasn't been sewn back on yet
Those outgrown clothes you meant to give to your sister
To-do lists with unchecked boxes
A book you don't know the ending to
The materials for a science project that you haven't quite started yet

There are many reasons why people don't finish what they start. One reason is a secret fear of failure. After all, if you don't finish something, then you can't technically fail at it! Instead, you might tuck your attempts away from judging eyes or wait until the last minute so that you can blame your ho-hum performance on a lack of time.

But God isn't like that with His children. When He begins His work in you, you can have faith that He will not fail. He is slowly perfecting you and will bring you to completion! And since God never gives up on you, you never have to fear failure in yourself, either.

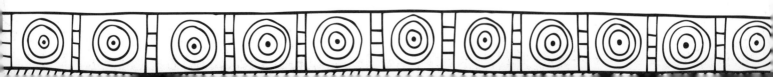

JESUS NEVER CHANGES

Jesus Christ is the same yesterday, today, and forever.

—Hebrews 13:8

The world is constantly changing.
In a single day, you could experience a change in

weather,	money,	pizza topping preferences,
hair color,	grades,	favorite movies,
mood,	routes to school,	houses, or
friendships,	boyfriends,	health.

When you stop to think about it, it's enough to make your head spin!
But there is someone who *never* changes: Jesus.

You can depend on His words to remain true. You can rely on Him to keep His promises. You can trust Him to never leave or forsake you.

Even as your world is shifting like crazy, He is steadfast. His love for you remains constant.

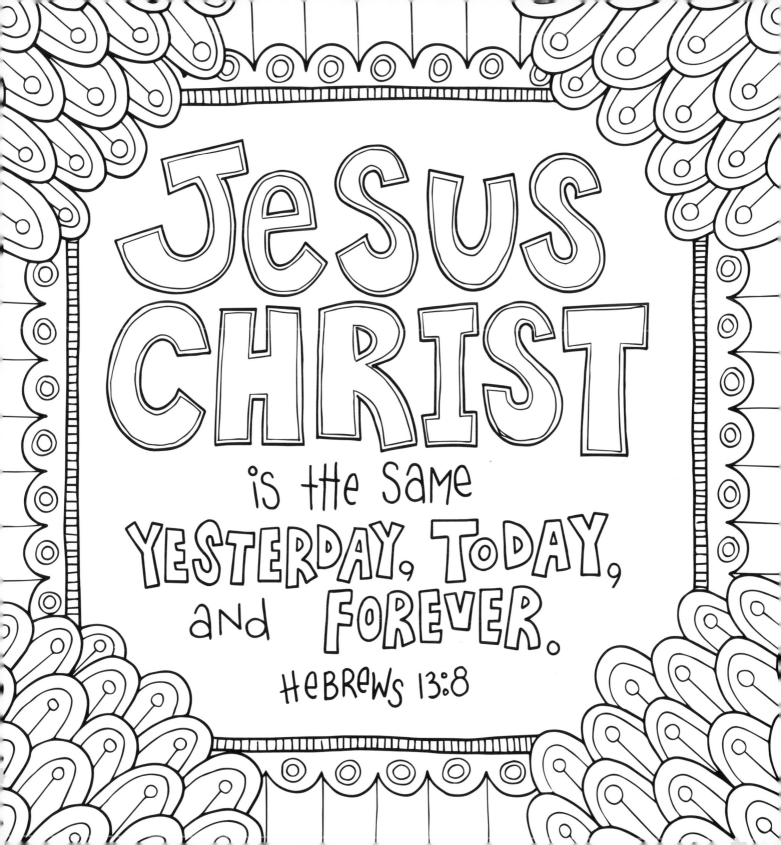

NO CONDEMNATION

There is no condemnation for those who belong to Christ Jesus.

—Romans 8:1

Oh, the perils of a Monopoly game.

You're rounding the game board with your little metal shoe. You're buying and selling property, getting ahead. You've got a big pile of money, just ready for you to swoop in and buy Boardwalk. You might win!

Suddenly, you pull the dreaded "Go Directly to Jail" card. *Grrrrrr.*

And there you sit, behind bars, while your friends continue to collect rent and get further and further ahead. Jail is not fun.

Do you put yourself in your own emotional jail when you make a mistake? Do you tell yourself that you're a failure who can't do anything right?

Satan loves it when we beat ourselves up for our mistakes and place ourselves in an emotional jail, away from God. When we do that, we place the focus on ourselves rather than on the huge sacrifice that Jesus made by dying on the cross and atoning for our sins.

We need to remember that there is no condemnation for those who belong to Jesus. If we have sinned, we can repent and turn back to God. We can also forgive ourselves, just as He forgives us. There is no need to stay trapped in our emotional jails—we have freedom in Christ!

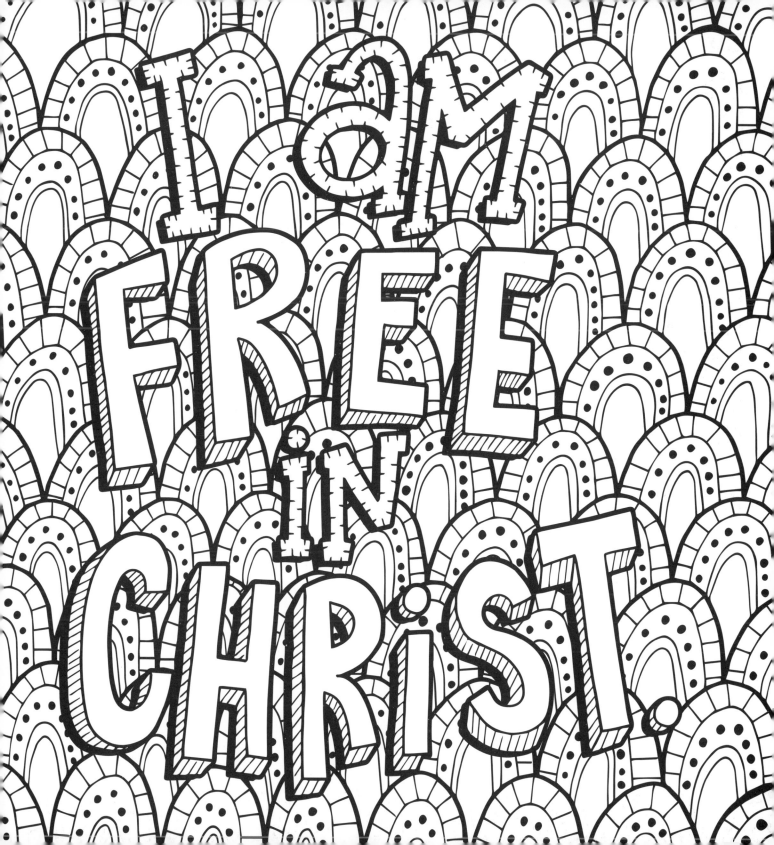

PRACTICE GRATITUDE

Always be joyful. Never stop praying. Be thankful in all circumstances, for this is God's will for you who belong to Christ Jesus.

—1 Thessalonians 5:16-18

We all get annoyed sometimes.

We get mad at the slow car in front of us, the gum we just stepped in, that girl whose hair never seems to frizz, the rain that won't stop, our brother who hogs the computer, the locker that constantly jams.

But if we stop and think about our irritation, we'll usually find that our funk is really about our own selfishness. We want things the way *we* want them, and we don't want to be inconvenienced. We don't want to be slowed down. We want things that are better, newer, shinier, prettier, bigger, louder, and fancier than what we have.

Our selfishness makes us grouchy.

So how can we break loose from our grouchiness?

The surefire way to combat a bad attitude is with gratitude! It's nearly impossible to stay bitter when you're counting the blessings God has showered upon you. One practical solution is to sit down and write a gratitude list. It doesn't have to be very long—just long enough to get your focus off yourself and on all your wonderful gifts from God.

What are you thankful for today? Friends? Creativity? Hamsters?

Take time today to thank God for His many gifts.

Be THANKFUL
in all circumstances.
1 Thessalonians 5:18

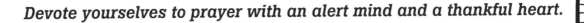

PRAY FIRST

Devote yourselves to prayer with an alert mind and a thankful heart.

—Colossians 4:2

A lot of things change once you turn sixteen and start driving. One of your new responsibilities is keeping track of your car keys.

And it just seems to happen that once a week or so . . . they are nowhere to be found.

Where could they be?

At the bottom of your purse? In your jacket pocket? In your freezer?

(Hopefully not in your locked car . . . *ugh.*)

And then, when you are about to start pulling your hair out, you find them. Usually in the most obvious place.

"They're always in the last place you look!" someone says.

Well, *of course* they're always in the last place you look. You don't keep looking for your keys after you've found them. Finding your keys solves your problem!

Are you approaching your struggles in the same manner as your lost keys? Are you searching every which way for solutions to your problems? Asking the advice of good friends and not-so-good friends? Taking cues from movie characters? Asking Google?

Or do you turn to God first?

Prayer should not be the last place that we turn in times of difficulty or confusion. God has all the answers. We could save ourselves a lot of frustration and grief if we turn to God *first,* instead of as a last resort.

And—unlike with your lost keys—you know where you should be looking right from the start.

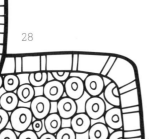

THE NAME OF THE LORD

The name of the Lord is a strong fortress;
the godly run to him and are safe.

—Proverbs 18:10

The world can be a pretty terrifying place.

All it takes to remind us of that is a click of the TV remote or a glance at our news feeds. Natural disasters come with no warning. People make hateful choices, devastating everyone around them. Bullying and greed and violence seem to be everywhere.

Sometimes the world's sin feels like too much for our weak hearts to handle. It seems that there is nothing we can do to stop the wrongdoing and calamity.

When we find ourselves frozen in fear or dread, there is one thing we *can* do. It is a small action that brings huge peace. We can take a moment and speak the name of the One who loves us best:

Jesus.

It doesn't have to be loud—just a faint whisper is enough. It's the call of our hearts to the One who is in control of this world.

The name of Jesus brings hope. His presence brings peace.

God knows our fears and struggles in this fallen world. But remember that He is in charge. Take courage—He has overcome the world.

THE NAME OF THE LORD is a STRONG FORTRESS.
PROVERBS 18:10

TRY NEW ADVENTURES

I can do everything through Christ, who gives me strength.

—Philippians 4:13

Often, God asks us to leave our comfort zones. He never lets us get stuck in a rut for too long!

Some of us are extroverts. Maybe the hard thing that God is calling us to do is to hang back and be quiet before Him. Spend time alone in prayer. Work in the background.

Some of us are introverts. We might be called to stand up and talk to a large group of people. Sing in front of a crowd. Make a new friend.

Of course, God doesn't want us to be someone we're not. He made us each special with our own unique gifts for a reason! He has a purpose for each of us. But sometimes He wants us to grow in our faith, and usually that means trying things that don't come easily to us—and learning to trust Him every step of the way.

God's goal for us is not our personal comfort. His goal is for us to grow every day, so that we might look more like His beloved Son, Jesus.

So what new thing is God calling *you* to do? No matter what it is, always remember that you can do all things through Christ, who gives you strength.

WAITING

Wait patiently for the LORD.
Be brave and courageous.
Yes, wait patiently for the LORD.

—Psalm 27:14

Waiting is tough, whether it is waiting for

the polish to absolutely, totally, completely dry on your fingernails,
the cat to wake up so you can move your legs again,
this boring play to be over so you can go home,
those scary test results to be posted,
your hair to grow past your shoulders,
the snow to start falling (or to stop falling),
that floppy-haired boy to notice you,
your parents to wake up so you can start unwrapping the presents,
your skills to catch up to the big ideas in your head,
the final book in the trilogy to be published, or
your broken heart to heal.

But sometimes the things we yearn for are not actually the best things for us. Sometimes, while waiting, we discover that our desires have changed. We might discover that God had a better plan for us all along. So what can we do?

We can live life one day at a time, seeking the Lord in our today and trusting Him with our tomorrows. God is in control, and He holds the future in His hands. If we seek the Lord, we can be sure that He will be good to us every step of the way.

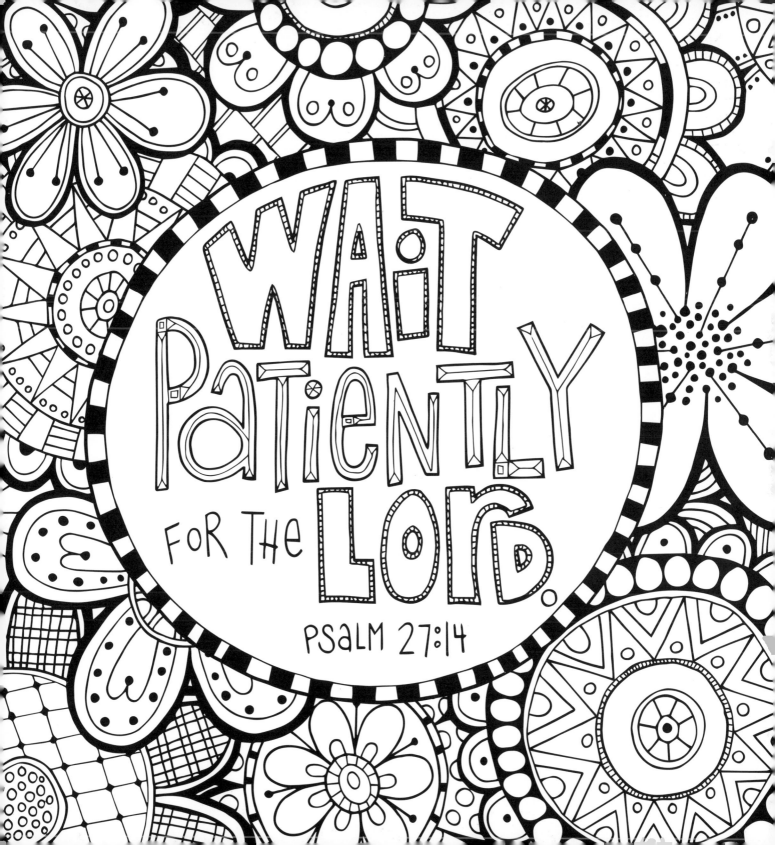

WAIT PATIENTLY FOR THE LORD.

PSALM 27:14

KEEP DOING GOOD

Let's not get tired of doing what is good. At just the right time we will reap a harvest of blessing if we don't give up.

—Galatians 6:9

Do you love building sand castles?

Sometimes it can take an entire afternoon—toting water from the shore, scooping and digging and sculpting. You craft turrets and moats, and make gardens with the algae you found floating in the waves. You work and build and persevere. When it's finished, you stand back and admire your beautiful creation.

And then the tide comes in . . . and your sand castle is washed away without a trace. *Sigh.*

Building a sand castle can be frustrating.

Choosing to do the right thing can be frustrating as well.

Every time we speak the truth, help someone in need, or share the Good News about Jesus, we are making a choice to do good in this world. But sometimes, despite our pure motives, things don't turn out the way we planned. Our efforts aren't noticed. Our attempts to start a friendship are rejected. Maybe we're even teased for trying. After all our hard work, we're not even certain if we made a bit of a difference.

But when we are choosing what God has asked us to do, we can rest assured that our work has not been in vain. Whether or not we ever see the results, God will use our work in His own way, in His own time, for His own glory.

It will not be washed away.

WHEN IN DOUBT, CHOOSE LOVE

[Jesus said,] "I am giving you a new commandment: Love each other. Just as I have loved you, you should love each other."

—John 13:34

Our days are filled with hundreds of small choices:

Eggs or cereal?
Curly or straightened hair?
Left or right?

One decision runs into the next. All of these tiny decisions add up to one big day. We are also faced with many more important choices every day:

Frown or smile?
Reject or invite?
Hold a grudge or forgive?

Our decisions can either tear down or build up our relationships with others.

Jesus greatly valued relationships, and He showed love in a variety of ways. He catered each interaction to the specific person He was trying to reach.

Sometimes He was gentle and tender. At other times, He was tough and asked challenging questions. Often, He had to speak the truth pointedly to reach a stubborn person's hardened heart.

In each of our relationships, we can look to Jesus' example. We can ask ourselves, "How would Jesus respond? How would Jesus show love to this person?"

When we look to Him and follow His ways, we can best show love to those around us.

SHINE YOUR LIGHT

Once you were full of darkness, but now you have light from the Lord. So live as people of light!

—Ephesians 5:8

You don't realize just how dark the night can be until you go camping.

During the daytime, you probably don't pay much attention to your flashlight. You're too busy hammering stakes for your tent, plumping up your sleeping bag, and collecting firewood so that you can roast s'mores later.

But when the sun goes down and darkness comes, you can bet that you'll begin rummaging around in your backpack for that flashlight.

Out in the woods, the night hides creepy-crawlies and rascally raccoons, not to mention low-lying branches that are just waiting to whack you in the face. When it comes time for that midnight bathroom run, you won't get far without a flashlight! If you don't have one, you'll need to depend on someone else who has light to help guide you through the woods.

As Christians, we are called to shine the light of Jesus into the darkness of the world, sort of like "spiritual flashlights." When we act like Jesus would, our light shines bright to expose lies, corruption, and evil, and shows the radical difference living for Christ makes. God's love and truth will always drive out the creepy-crawlies of deception and sin.

So stand boldly and let your light shine bright!

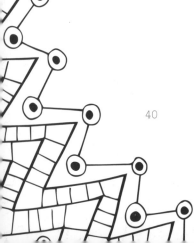

BEAUTY FOR ASHES

To all who mourn in Israel,
*   he will give a crown of beauty for ashes,*
a joyous blessing instead of mourning,
*   festive praise instead of despair.*
In their righteousness, they will be like great oaks
*   that the LORD has planted for his own glory.*

—Isaiah 61:3

Have you ever looked into a fire pit the morning after a bonfire?

It's usually full of powdery ashes, blackened shards of branches, and dirty remnants of gooey marshmallow-roasting sticks. The logs, once solid tree trunks, smolder all night long until only soot and cinders remain. A bonfire's flames turn anything they touch into ruins. You could use the best glue in the universe, but you'd never get those ashes looking like wood again! Those logs are hopelessly incinerated.

We, too, were once hopeless before Christ entered our lives. We were lost to sin and stuck in our own selfishness and despair. We were a real mess!

But our God is in the business of radical transformation. God loves to show His glory by taking the hopeless and bringing hope, and by making the impossible possible. God can take your broken soul and make it whole again. In fact, He can make it even better!

No matter how hot your mess, God can take the grubby ashes of your life and create something beautiful.

42

CLEAN HEART

Create in me a clean heart, O God.
Renew a loyal spirit within me.

—Psalm 51:10

Sweat, grime, and dirt are some of the drawbacks in the life of an athletic girl.

Let's say you're at soccer practice and before you know it, you're caked in mud. Your cleats are two big mud pies, and your hair is a stringy mess. When you get home, your mother takes one look at you and says, "No way are you traipsing through the house like *that*!" So you're banished to the laundry room, where you deposit your mucky clothes in the washing machine and then head straight to the shower—not touching anything along the way! Only once you are clean—with shampooed hair and wearing sweet-smelling clothes—are you free to join the rest of your family at the kitchen table for dinner.

The filth of sin is much more serious than the dirt of a soccer field. Sin does more than just separate us from our loved ones; it separates us from God.

But God craves to be with us! He doesn't want us to sit on the sidelines, too muddy and sinful to play. He wants us to turn to Him, ask for forgiveness, and allow Him to wash us clean.

Is there an area in your life that you need God to make clean? Bring it to Him today. He longs to do it.

GIFTS

God has given each of you a gift from his great variety of spiritual gifts. Use them well to serve one another.

—1 Peter 4:10

Say you're stranded on a desert island . . .

Every day, you wait for help to arrive.

Finally, one day, a huge crate washes up on the shore. Holding your breath, you open it. You peer inside and find thousands of wooden toothpicks, rolls of duct tape, and stacks of Styrofoam cups.

Do you complain because you weren't given a prepackaged kayak with step-by-step instructions? No! You use what you have and set out to build the sturdiest toothpick boat you possibly can!

In life, we don't get to choose the gifts that God gives us, either.

You might not have been given a commanding speaking voice, organizational skills, or leadership abilities. When you sing, all the animals might run for the hills. But God has definitely given you a special gift to be used for His Kingdom.

Think for a moment. What gives you joy? What are you passionate about?

Are you good with kids? Do you like to bake cakes? Would you enjoy playing chess with a lonely grandparent? Do you have compassion for homeless animals? God can use you.

Do not mourn what you do not have. Instead, rejoice in what you have been given!

SOLID INSIDE

You should clothe yourselves instead with the beauty that comes from within, the unfading beauty of a gentle and quiet spirit, which is so precious to God.

—1 Peter 3:4

Russia is famous for *matryoshka* dolls, also called nesting dolls. These wooden dolls, each with a smaller one placed inside it, are unique works of art. Traditionally, they are painted as little peasant women, dressed in traditional clothing.

Within each set of dolls, at the very center, lies the smallest baby doll. Although the larger *matryoshka* dolls are elaborately decorated with ornate flowers and patterns, the baby is much simpler in design. She also is not hollow like the others, but made of solid wood. She is tiny but special.

Sometimes we forget that what is truly important is our innermost self. The world places great emphasis on outer appearances: model-like bodies, stylish clothes, and trendy hairstyles. But, like *matryoshka* dolls, our bodies weather over time. Our teeth might chip; our skin might scar and wrinkle. Our clothing may rip, fray, or go out of style. And all it takes is a few months for our new hairstyle to become yesterday's trend!

But when God shapes our innermost being, none of that matters. If our souls are focused on God and letting Him shape us, our cores will remain solid and beautiful. It's what lies inside us that is most pleasing to God—a gentle heart that seeks Him.

CLOTHE YOURSELVES instead with the BEAUTY THAT COMES FROM WITHIN. 1 Peter 3:4

FIX YOUR THOUGHTS

Fix your thoughts on what is true, and honorable, and right, and pure, and lovely, and admirable. Think about things that are excellent and worthy of praise.

—Philippians 4:8

Have you ever twirled around on a tire swing?

You twist the rope tightly, all the way up to the branch. You hold your breath and let go, spinning like a top. You watch the tree trunk, your picnic table, and your patio whip around you until, at last, you slow to a halt.

Finally, you hop off the swing—and promptly fall flat on your face from dizziness. (Hopefully nobody was there to see it!)

Dancers have to train themselves to combat dizziness, especially when performing *piqué* turns and *pirouettes*. One technique they use is called "spotting." If dancers were to concentrate on everything whirling around them while they spun, their brains would become overloaded and confused with mixed messages. Instead, they stay balanced by keeping their eyes oriented on one spot.

We could learn a lot from those dancers.

In life, it's easy for us to get distracted from the truth. There are arguments, lies, criticism, and hatred all around us. If we aren't careful, those negative thoughts can get stuck in our heads! It's important to be careful what we "spot" our minds on. What is in our minds affects our hearts and souls. And what's in our souls affects our entire lives.

Fix your thoughts on what is true, pure, and good. Fix your thoughts on Jesus.

THIS TOO SHALL PASS

Even when I walk
*   through the darkest valley,*
I will not be afraid,
*   for you are close beside me.*
Your rod and your staff
*   protect and comfort me.*

—Psalm 23:4

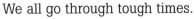

We all go through tough times.

In the book of Psalms, David talks about walking through the darkest valley, with the shadow of fear and death hanging over him. And, boy, did he ever have some rough times! From his youth as a poor shepherd to his mighty position as the king of Israel, David faced many trials: an unequally matched clash with a giant, torment from King Saul, and his own personal battle with sin.

Riches, fame, and privilege cannot shield us from the troubles of life. Whether you are an anonymous high-school student or a social-media sensation, not one person is immune.

But though you must walk through the dark valleys in life, you don't have to set up camp in them. You may have to weather the hard season, but God will walk you through to the other side.

Just as David points out, God will give us the support we need along the way: comfort, joy, strength, and peace. He can sculpt and refine us in that desolate place. There, He can build compassion, character, and even humor and joy in us.

Jesus never promised that we would be trouble-free in this world. In fact, He promises the opposite. But He also promises us His peace. Whatever dark valley you are facing in life, God will be there with you.

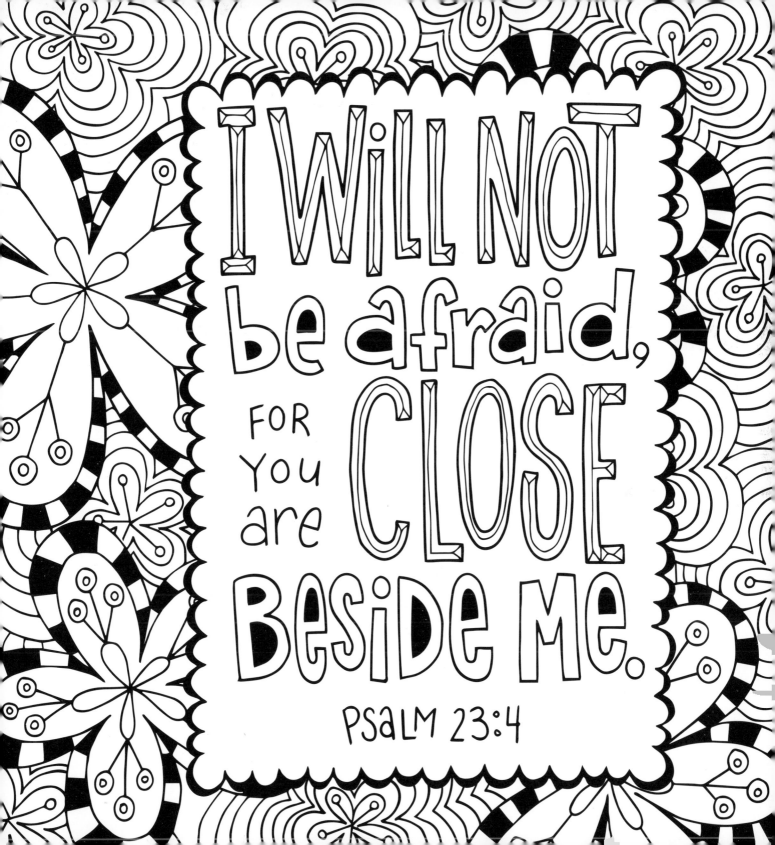

I WILL NOT be afraid, for you are CLOSE Beside me.

Psalm 23:4

Trust in the LORD with all your heart;
do not depend on your own understanding.

—Proverbs 3:5

Suppose you woke up one morning and said, "Hey! I think I'll drive from New York to California today!"

Then you run to your car, throw an extra pair of socks in the glove compartment, and take off. Directions? What directions? You don't need directions! It would just ruin all your fun, right? So off you go—with no smartphone, GPS, or map.

Well, guess what?

Chances are that you'd get good and lost. It's highly likely that you'd end up stranded on the Appalachian Trail, stuck in a Florida swamp, or driving in circles in the Canadian wilderness. In fact, you might not even make it out of your city.

Let's face it: you don't have all the information. You don't know the way.

Often, we do the same thing in our personal lives without even knowing it. We think, "Hey, I'm gonna do what I want. I've got this!" without ever stopping to ask God to reveal *His* will for us. When we forge ahead without consulting God, we are traveling without a much-needed map.

God has all the information. *All* of it. He knows the past, the future, the tiny details, the big picture, and everything in between. He knows more than our minds can even begin to comprehend.

Ask Him to lead you, and you will never be lost.

GOD'S MASTERPIECE

We are God's masterpiece. He has created us anew in Christ Jesus, so we can do the good things he planned for us long ago.

—Ephesians 2:10

How awesome it is to enter an art museum and be greeted with a glorious feast for the eyes! Each piece of artwork is wonderfully unique, from the smallest watercolor to the largest sculpture. There's

simple art and head-scratching art;
make-you-laugh art and make-you-cry art;
sensible, reasonable, useful art and entirely impractical art;
thousands-of-years-old art and just-made-today art;
clean, crisp, neat art and stinky, muddy, dirty art;
small, delicate, whispery art and big, bold, loud art;
on-purpose art and accidental art;
realistic art and weird art.

Just as each artist has a vision for his or her artwork, God has a specific design for His creations. Each one of us is different and beautiful in our own way, created for a certain purpose.

Like the artwork in a museum, we might be too simple or bold or weird or thought-provoking for some people to handle. Some people might scratch their heads when we open our mouths. (Sometimes, we might even confuse ourselves.) But God had a special reason for creating you, and He always understands you. So trust that He's got great plans for your life.

Celebrate your creation! You are God's work of art.

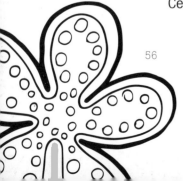

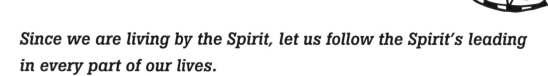

EXTRA BRAKES

Since we are living by the Spirit, let us follow the Spirit's leading in every part of our lives.

—Galatians 5:25

If you've ever taken a driver's ed course, you may have realized that the training cars are unique. On the driver's side of the car, everything is just as it is on a normal car. But on the floorboard on the passenger's side, there's another brake pedal.

Why?

The passenger's seat is where the driving instructor sits. The instructor can see the dangers ahead that newbie driving eyes might miss, like a stop sign hidden behind a branch or a small dog crossing the road. If the student gets a bit too confident and starts driving too fast, the instructor can slow the car down. The student learns to drive and navigate, but the instructor is still in control.

Sometimes we start moving a bit too fast in our own lives. We might start hanging out with the wrong crowd or experimenting with unhealthy behaviors. Even a brief flirtation with sin can get us way off track.

But if we have the Holy Spirit in our lives, we have a loving navigator to guide and protect us. He might have to slam on the brakes right before we careen out of control. However, if we listen to His quiet voice before things get dangerous, there might not be a need for screeching tires, inflated air bags, and painful consequences. We can learn to listen for His leading as He gently pushes us in the direction that we should go.

Let's quiet our hearts and wait intently for His leading.

DON'T COPY!

Don't copy the behavior and customs of this world, but let God transform you into a new person by changing the way you think. Then you will learn to know God's will for you, which is good and pleasing and perfect.

—Romans 12:2

If you've ever made a photocopy, you might have noticed that the paper contained smudges and ink marks. Smudges happen when little pieces of dust land on the glass screen of the copier. And the random ink splotches are from running the paper through the workings of a dirty machine. The copy might not be crystal clear, but it'll do.

But if you take that photocopy and make another copy, the new copy will be muddier and grainier. It might start to get a little tough to read. And if you make a copy of a copy of a copy of a copy of a copy of a copy of a copy of a copy, there's a good chance that you won't be able to tell what the words or images even are!

As Christians, we are called to *not* copy the way the world does things. If we start copying the world, our light slowly starts to get muddier and muddier, until there's nothing left to see at all. If our light is dimmed, how can others see Jesus in us?

Are there some ways that you're copying the world?

Using God's name disrespectfully?
Making mean, sarcastic jokes?
Wearing inappropriate clothing?
Watching television shows that bring you down?

Today, make a choice to be transformed. Choose God's ways instead of the world's habits. Be different!

BURDENS

Share each other's burdens, and in this way obey the law of Christ.

—Galatians 6:2

Did you know that an ant can carry fifty times its own body weight (and perhaps even more)?

If you could accomplish this feat, you wouldn't have to worry about the math book in your backpack, because you could lift a Volkswagen Beetle. Maybe even two!

But you are not an ant, and you are not meant to carry small cars over your head. You're also not meant to carry heavy emotional burdens by yourself.

You might be dealing with some very difficult hardships: the loss of a loved one, anxiety over the future, fear of failure, deep loneliness, or depression. Though these burdens may not be visible from the outside, they can weigh heavily on your soul.

During these times, you may feel very alone. But you are not alone! You are part of God's family. We are meant to help carry one another's burdens by listening, encouraging, and praying. And when we carry someone else's burdens, it often makes our own burdens seem much lighter.

Are you burdened today? Who can you reach out to? Can you take a load off of someone else's shoulders?

Life is better when we care for one another.